BANJO PATERSON'S
AUSTRALIANS

BANJO PATERSON'S
AUSTRALIANS

Selected Poems and Prose by A. B. Paterson   *Paintings by Dorothy Gauvin*

ANGUS
& ROBERTSON
PUBLISHERS

ANGUS & ROBERTSON PUBLISHERS

Unit 4, Eden Park, 31 Waterloo Road,
North Ryde, NSW, Australia 2113;
94 Newton Road, Auckland 1,
New Zealand; and
16 Golden Square, London WIR 4BN,
United Kindgdom

First published in Australia
by Angus & Robertson Publishers in 1989
First published in New Zealand
by Angus & Robertson NZ Ltd in 1989

National Library of Australia
Cataloguing-in-publication data

Paterson, A.B. (Andrew Barton), 1864-1941.
   Banjo Paterson's Australians.

   ISBN 0 207 16190 9.

   I. Gauvin, Dorothy. II. Title.

A821'.2

Typeset By Midland Typesetters
Printed in Australia by Griffin Press

CONTENTS

BANJO PATERSON'S AUSTRALIANS

A. B. "Banjo" Paterson

Born in 1864 near Orange, New South Wales, Andrew Barton Paterson was the eldest child of Andrew Bogle Paterson and his wife Rose Isabella. After the failure of their grazing ventures in the Orange area and in Queensland, the family moved to a station called Illalong, near Yass. That too failed, and the property was sold, but the purchaser agreed to employ Paterson's father to manage it. Thus young "Barty" Paterson passed most of his youth at Illalong, and the property and surrounding districts were to provide the inspiration for much of his work. Here he met the prototypes of some of the bush characters that people the verses in this collection, and developed the respect for horses and horsemanship that became so much a feature of his work.

Paterson's first published poem appeared in the *Bulletin* in 1885, when he was twenty-one years old. The first of his ballads to attract significant attention, however, was "Old Pardon, the Son of Reprieve", which appeared in the *Bulletin*'s pages in 1888 under the pseudonym "The Banjo" (a name that Paterson had taken from one of Illalong's station horses). Other poems were published over the succeeding years, to ever-wider acclaim, and a selection was eventually presented in book form in 1895, when Angus & Robertson published *The Man from Snowy River and Other Verses* and revealed for the first time the identity of the mysterious "Banjo". Since that time, while the popularity of other balladists' work may have waned, Paterson's place in the affections of his countrymen has remained as sure as ever.

Paterson's most prolific period as a poet was during his twenties and thirties, when he produced many of the timeless pieces included here. But, although best remembered as the author of poems like "The Man from Snowy River", "The Man from Ironbark", "A Bush Christening" and "Mulga Bill's Bicycle", he was also a well-respected journalist and editor. From October 1899 to July 1900 he acted as a war correspondent, reporting on the Boer War for Australian newspapers, and, though trained as a solicitor, he thereafter turned his back on a law career to make his living from his pen. For a time he wrote feature articles for Sydney newspapers and was then appointed editor of *The Evening News*.

Paterson seems to have been torn between his enjoyment of the life of a Sydney writer and his love of the Australian bush. In 1908 he decided to return to the land, and, with his wife and two children, moved to a property on the fringes of Snowy River country, then later took over a wheat farm at Grenfell. On the outbreak of World War I, however, Paterson abandoned farming to serve first as an ambulance driver in France and later as a Lieutenant in the AIF, rising to the rank of Major. After the war he returned to his career in journalism, and was still working as a freelance writer until just before his death at the age of seventy-six.

From his wide experience, Paterson wrote about city life and bush life, about sporting life and service life, but, above all, he wrote about people, ordinary people. Drovers and drinkers and sportsmen, farmers and soldiers and clowns, bushmen newly arrived in the city and English toffs facing life outback—these are the folk who are presented with affection and humour in Paterson's most memorable work, and today the resourceful and defiant Australians whom he immortalised are seen as symbols of the nation's character.

BANJO PATERSON'S AUSTRALIANS

DOROTHY GAUVIN

Dorothy Gauvin was born in Winton, Queensland, where A. B. Paterson wrote the words of "Waltzing Matilda". In 1984, after numerous successful group and solo exhibitions, the artist made an extensive personal study tour of the great galleries of Europe. Returning to Australia, she began work on the theme she has made uniquely her own—the on-going series based on the characters who appear in "The Banjo's" poems and prose.

Thirty-three paintings from the series appeared in *Banjo Paterson's People* (Angus & Robertson Publishers, 1987), and the present collection comprises a further thirty-three works. About the series in general and the paintings in this collection, Dorothy Gauvin says:

Most Australians hold deep in their hearts a belief that Australia is the Bush, and have an image of the Australian as a man on horseback, alone on the trackless plain.

The reality is, for me, a much richer tapestry of lives led by ordinary men and women, in the towns as well as in the open spaces. The barber and the bartender seem as interesting to me as the cattle king and the outlaw. The lives of the women, sketched in so lightly by history, seem to me like the veins of colour in opal matrix, only glimpsed beneath the overlaying ironstone.

The qualities and values of these people formed the mould from which our national identity is cast. The ability to improvise from what's at hand; the laconic humour within which heroic deeds become "all in a day's work"; the ingrained loyalty of "never let your mates down"; above all the willingness to "have a go"—these are the foundation stones of the Australian character.

Adrift in troubled times, it may be this strength of character, this sense of national identity which can be our liferaft. This is the theme which connects all of the paintings in this series.

Like any true artist, "Banjo" Paterson rewards those who look beneath the surface of his work. Often, a wise comment on human nature or a lovely joke will be half-hidden in the rollicking lines of his bush ballads. A case in point is "Father Riley's Horse".

Over the years I'd read the poem "Father Riley's Horse" several times, always taking the story at face value. When I came to visualising the painting "The Horse Thief", I kept seeing a sly grin passing between the priest and the hunted man. This seemed quite wrong for the story, so I went back to the poem. Reading it again, it became clear that my subconscious had been kicking me to see the joke Paterson had hidden between the lines. No Irish priest worth his salt would turn one of his flock in to the Law, and it's clear that Andy has come to the end of his rope. The dreaded "traps" are close on his trail. So a clever ruse is worked out to save Andy and, just incidentally, to make a bundle to benefit the poor. Andy will "die" and be duly "buried" by the parish priest, who has quite recently acquired a new horse of dubious parentage. Entering this rank outsider in the local races, the good Father accepts the odds in a spirit of Christian charity. Alone of the populace, the old dog poisoner (who camps at night beside the racetrack) bets on Father Riley's horse to win. His cash reward after the race is due less to his spiritual faith than to his canny powers of observation and deductive reasoning.

"Firepower" is a painting that deals with a much more serious subject. The disastrous effects of the Depression which began with the financial collapse of Argentina in 1890 were exacerbated in Australia by militant action taken by the newly federated labour Unions. The Great Shearer's Strike of 1891 led on to even more violent action by striking shearers and other bush workers in 1893. By 1894 a large area of western Queensland was under martial law. In July and August alone, eight woolsheds, often containing the entire woolclip, had been burnt by the strikers protesting the use of "free" or non-

union shearers. On 2 September, sixteen unionists beseiged Dagworth station, keeping the "squatter" and his men pinned down under a hail of gunfire while one of their number set fire to the woolshed. It seemed a deadly business, yet during two years of armed confrontation, it's notable that there were only two casualties—one unionist who suicided after the burning of Dagworth, another who was shot by a fellow unionist after an argument. It is in reference to this that I've given my happy arsonist the loony, mischievous grin of a larrikin out on a lark, blissfully unaware of the serious consequences of the striking of that match.

For some years, I'd been fascinated by the idea of making a painting which would revolve around a game of billiards. Now, like all artists, I'm affected by the images made by other artists before me and so, each time I approached Paterson's "Hay, Hell and Booligal", my mind filled with the well-known pictures of rough characters swilling their grog and having a wonderful ding-dong around the billiards table. Finally, the scenario I imagined for the two paintings based on this very funny poem involves a mob of cattle just delivered to a run in the district. The boss drover and his men naturally head for the pub to cut out their cheques. I decided that this could well be one of those almost palatial establishments which graced many a small town in that era. In my imagination, the pub is owned and run by an elegant widow whose success is evidenced by the opulent furnishings, including the gas-fed chandeliers and beautiful ceramic and brass beer pulls which were then commonplace. Billiards being the only sport in town, it's not long before honour demands that the boss drover must extend a challenge to the local champion, a well-to-do squatter with time on his hands. It's your guess which of the two won the match. Or is the real winner the astute proprietor of the pub? She knows the game will be endlessly post-mortemed, the arguments washed down with copious draughts of her golden brew.

You will notice that in the painting "The Visiting Priest", the only element that is distinctively Australian is the blue cattle dog. The Smithfield, well established by 1830, was developed by various stages to the familiar type seen here, officially recognised in 1890. Apart from the dog, this cottage could be set anywhere in western Europe or north America of the time, as styles changed very slowly and those changes travelled even more slowly to frontier countries like the Australia of last century.

By 1893, the worldwide Depression had caused widespread unemployment in Australia. Thousands of men were forced to roll their swags and travel the roads, seeking work. Even the small cash relief provided by the embattled Government was advanced on a once-only basis at each centre. So most "swagmen" moved ever further on, further away from the families they'd left behind. Like so many others, the young wife depicted in "The Letter' waits for word from her travelling man, their only link the infrequent and uncertain arrival of the mail. Once more she reads his latest letter as she watches the leaves fall from the English maples and longs for the day when they will be reunited.

When the drawing for "Mining the Swagman's Rest" was completed, for some reason I couldn't explain, I left it for three days without applying the fixative. This is a bit dicey, for the charcoal is very soft and vulnerable to obliteration if accidentally rubbed against. It was a lucky thing though, because my husband then phoned to say, "Grab your camera and sketchbook and get yourself downtown—they're setting up an old gold stamper in front of the hotel!" This was manna from heaven, as I'd been struggling to decipher, with the aid of only written descriptions from the Britannica, the photographs of an abandoned gold stamper a friend had brought back from his travels in the Gulf country. Now I could actually touch one, it ended up as the centrepiece of this painting which shows a range of equipment, provided by an amateur prospector friend, as used by gold miners before the era of mechanisation on the large scale we know today. The waterlily (lotus) and the brolga (crane) suggest the everlasting spirit of the swagman whose memorial is carved into the living bloodwood which shades his final resting place.

Living beside the Great Barrier Reef, I was delighted to discover a way of showing, not only the beauties of this tropical ocean with its undersea gardens, but also one of the modern breed of divers who makes his living working on or beneath its waters. In striking contrast to the early divers who thought only of harvesting the reefs' bounty, the subject of "Today's Diver" is a dedicated researcher with the DPI Northern Fisheries Research station.

Paterson's essay "The Merino Sheep" would have to be one of the funniest pieces of writing ever produced on this subject. Yet, in "Starting the End Run", what I've endeavoured to depict is a concentrated history of wool transport in Australia in the era before the introduction of steam shipping.

The finale of a mini-series of paintings inspired by the poem "The Man from Ironbark", "The Joke's Over!" was completed almost four years after the others in its set. For the series, I'd invented a young apprentice to the wise-cracking barber and here he is shown trying to revive his boss, felled by the infuriated bushie. All the elements involved in the previous four paintings (which can be seen in Banjo Paterson's People) come together in this final piece. Even the barber's chair is unveiled, this being based on a fine example I saw in a historical museum at Charters Towers. The models had such a good time posing for this picture that proceedings were often held up by fits of laughter, particularly when the family cat decided that the chest of the prone barber was the ideal nesting spot and could not be dissuaded.

Gauvin oil paintings feature in numerous corporate and private collections throughout Australia, in Canada and in the USA.

The artist lives in Cairns, in tropical North Queensland, with her husband Carl Wellington and their son Paul. She is currently engaged in research for her third book of paintings reflecting her interest in Australia's history.

Mulga Bill's Bicycle

JULY 1896

'Twas Mulga Bill, from Eaglehawk, that caught the cycling craze;
He turned away the good old horse that served him many days;
He dressed himself in cycling clothes, resplendent to be seen;
He hurried off to town and bought a shining new machine;
And as he wheeled it through the door, with air of lordly pride,
The grinning shop assistant said, "Excuse me, can you ride?"

"See here, young man," said Mulga Bill, "from Walgett to the sea,
From Conroy's Gap to Castlereagh, there's none can ride like me.
I'm good all round at everything, as everybody knows,
Although I'm not the one to talk—I *hate* a man that blows.
But riding is my special gift, my chiefest, sole delight;
Just ask a wild duck can it swim, a wildcat can it fight.
There's nothing clothed in hair or hide, or built of flesh or steel,
There's nothing walks or jumps, or runs, on axle, hoof, or wheel,
But what I'll sit, while hide will hold and girths and straps are tight:
I'll ride this here two-wheeled concern right straight away at sight."

'Twas Mulga Bill, from Eaglehawk, that sought his own abode,
That perched above the Dead Man's Creek, beside the mountain road.
He turned the cycle down the hill and mounted for the fray,
But ere he'd gone a dozen yards it bolted clean away.
It left the track, and through the trees, just like a silver streak,
It whistled down the awful slope towards the Dead Man's Creek.

It shaved a stump by half an inch, it dodged a big white-box:
The very wallaroos in fright went scrambling up the rocks,
The wombats hiding in their caves dug deeper underground,
As Mulga Bill, as white as chalk, sat tight to every bound.
It struck a stone and gave a spring that cleared a fallen tree,
It raced beside a precipice as close as close could be;
And then as Mulga Bill let out one last despairing shriek
It made a leap of twenty feet into the Dead Man's Creek.

'Twas Mulga Bill, from Eaglehawk, that slowly swam ashore:
He said, "I've had some narrer shaves and lively rides before;
I've rode a wild bull round a yard to win a five-pound bet,
But this was the most awful ride that I've encountered yet.
I'll give that two-wheeled outlaw best; it's shaken all my nerve
To feel it whistle through the air and plunge and buck and swerve.
It's safe at rest in Dead Man's Creek, we'll leave it lying still;
A horse's back is good enough henceforth for Mulga Bill."

THE SWAGMAN'S REST

OCTOBER 1895

We buried old Bob where the bloodwoods wave
    At the foot of the Eaglehawk;
We fashioned a cross on the old man's grave,
    For fear that his ghost might walk;
We carved his name on a bloodwood tree,
    With the date of his sad decease,
And in place of "Died from effects of spree",
    We wrote, "May he rest in peace".

For Bob was known on the Overland,
    A regular old bush wag,
Tramping along in the dust and sand,
    Humping his well worn swag.
He would camp for days in the river bed,
    And loiter and "fish for whales".
"I'm into the swagman's yard", he said,
    "And I never shall find the rails."

But he found the rails on that summer night
    For a better place—or worse,
As we watched by turns in the flickering light.
    With an old black gin for nurse.
The breeze came in with the scent of pine,
    The river sounded clear,
When a change came on, and we saw the sign
    That told us the end was near.

But he spoke in a cultured voice and low—
    "I fancy they've 'sent the route';
I once was an army man, you know,
    Though now I'm a drunken brute;

But bury me out where the bloodwoods wave,
    And if ever you're fairly stuck,
Just take and shovel me out of the grave,
    And, maybe, I'll bring you luck.

"For I've always heard—" here his voice fell weak,
    His strength was well-nigh sped,
He gasped and struggled and tried to speak,
    Then fell in a moment—dead.
Thus ended a wasted life and hard,
    Of energies misapplied—
Old Bob was out of the "swagman's yard"
    And over the Great Divide.

The drought came down on the field and flock,
    And never a raindrop fell,
Though the tortured moans of the starving stock
    Might soften a fiend from hell.
And we thought of the hint that the swagman gave
    When he went to the Great Unseen—
We shovelled the skeleton out of the grave
    To see what his hint might mean.

We dug where the cross and the graveposts were,
    We shovelled away the mould,
When sudden a vein of quartz lay bare
    All gleaming with yellow gold.
'Twas a reef with never a fault nor baulk
    That ran from the range's crest,
And the richest mine on the Eaglehawk
    Is known as "The Swagman's Rest".

BANJO PATERSON'S AUSTRALIANS

THE MAN FROM SNOWY RIVER

APRIL 1890

There was movement at the station, for the word had passed around
That the colt from old Regret had got away,
And had joined the wild bush horses—he was worth a thousand pound,
So all the cracks had gathered to the fray.
All the tried and noted riders from the stations near and far
Had mustered at the homestead overnight,
For the bushmen love hard riding where the wild bush horses are,
And the stockhorse snuffs the battle with delight.

There was Harrison, who made his pile when Pardon won the cup,
The old man with his hair as white as snow;
But few could ride beside him when his blood was fairly up—
He would go wherever horse and man could go.
And Clancy of the Overflow came down to lend a hand,
No better horseman ever held the reins;
For never horse could throw him while the saddle girths would stand,
He learnt to ride while droving on the plains.

And one was there, a stripling on a small and weedy beast,
He was something like a racehorse undersized,
With a touch of Timor pony—three parts thoroughbred at least—
And such as are by mountain horsemen prized.
He was hard and tough and wiry—just the sort that won't say die—
There was courage in his quick impatient tread;
And he bore the badge of gameness in his bright and fiery eye,
And the proud and lofty carriage of his head.

But still so slight and weedy, one would doubt his power to stay,
And the old man said, "That horse will never do
For a long and tiring gallop—lad, you'd better stop away,
Those hills are far too rough for such as you."
So he waited sad and wistful—only Clancy stood his friend—
"I think we ought to let him come," he said;
"I warrant he'll be with us when he's wanted at the end,
For both his horse and he are mountain bred.

"He hails from Snowy River, up by Kosciusko's side,
Where the hills are twice as steep and twice as rough,
Where a horse's hoofs strike firelight from the flint stones every stride,
The man that holds his own is good enough.
And the Snowy River riders on the mountains make their home,
Where the river runs those giant hills between;
I have seen full many horsemen since I first commenced to roam,
But nowhere yet such horsemen have I seen."

So he went—they found the horses by the big mimosa clump—
They raced away towards the mountain's brow,
And the old man gave his orders, "Boys, go at them from the jump,
No use to try for fancy riding now.
And, Clancy, you must wheel them, try and wheel them to the right.
Ride boldly, lad, and never fear the spills,
For never yet was rider that could keep the mob in sight,
If once they gain the shelter of those hills."

So Clancy rode to wheel them—he was racing on the wing
Where the best and boldest riders take their place,
And he raced his stockhorse past them, and he made the ranges ring
With the stockwhip, as he met them face to face.
Then they halted for a moment, while he swung the dreaded lash,
But they saw their well-loved mountain full in view,
And they charged beneath the stockwhip with a sharp and sudden dash,
And off into the mountain scrub they flew.

Then fast the horsemen followed, where the gorges deep and black
Resounded to the thunder of their tread,
And the stockwhips woke the echoes, and they fiercely answered back
From cliffs and crags that beetled overhead.
And upward, ever upward, the wild horses held their way,
Where mountain ash and kurrajong grew wide;
And the old man muttered fiercely, "We may bid the mob good day,
No man can hold them down the other side."

BANJO PATERSON'S AUSTRALIANS

11

BANJO PATERSON'S AUSTRALIANS

When they reached the mountain's summit, even Clancy took a pull,
It well might make the boldest hold their breath,
The wild hop scrub grew thickly, and the hidden ground was full
Of wombat holes, and any slip was death.
But the man from Snowy River let the pony have his head,
And he swung his stockwhip round and gave a cheer,
And he raced him down the mountain like a torrent down its bed,
While the others stood and watched in very fear.

He sent the flint stones flying, but the pony kept his feet,
He cleared the fallen timber in his stride,
And the man from Snowy River never shifted in his seat—
It was grand to see that mountain horseman ride.
Through the stringybarks and saplings, on the rough and broken ground,
Down the hillside at a racing pace he went;
And he never drew the bridle till he landed safe and sound,
At the bottom of that terrible descent.

He was right among the horses as they climbed the further hill,
And the watchers on the mountain standing mute,
Saw him ply the stockwhip fiercely, he was right among them still,
As he raced across the clearing in pursuit.

Then they lost him for a moment, where two mountain gullies met
In the ranges, but a final glimpse reveals
On a dim and distant hillside the wild horses racing yet,
With the man from Snowy River at their heels.

And he ran them single-handed till their sides were white with foam.
He followed like a bloodhound on their track,
Till they halted cowed and beaten, then he turned their heads for home,
And alone and unassisted brought them back.
But his hardy mountain pony he could scarcely raise a trot,
He was blood from hip to shoulder from the spur;
But his pluck was still undaunted, and his courage fiery hot,
For never yet was mountain horse a cur.

And down by Kosciusko, where the pine-clad ridges raise
Their torn and rugged battlements on high,
Where the air is clear as crystal, and the white stars fairly blaze
At midnight in the cold and frosty sky,
And where around The Overflow the reed beds sweep and sway
To the breezes, and the rolling plains are wide,
The man from Snowy River is a household word today,
And the stockmen tell the story of his ride.

"In re a Gentleman, One"

MARCH 1889

*When an attorney is called before the Full Court to answer for any alleged
misconduct it is not usual to publish his name until he is found guilty; until
then the matter appears in the papers, "In re a Gentleman, One of the
Attorneys of the Supreme Court," or, more shortly,
"In re a Gentleman, One."*

We see it each day in the paper,
   And know that there's mischief in store;
That some unprofessional caper
   Has landed a shark on the shore.
We know there'll be plenty of trouble
   Before they get through with the fun,
Because he's been coming the double
   On clients, has "Gentleman, One."

Alas! for the gallant attorney,
   Intent upon cutting a dash,
Sets out on life's perilous journey
   With rather more cunning than cash.
And fortune at first is inviting—
   He struts his brief hour in the sun—
But, lo! on the wall is the writing
   Of Nemesis, "Gentleman, One."

For soon he runs short of the dollars,
   He fears he must go to the wall;
So Peter's trust-money he collars
   To pay off his creditor, Paul;
Then robs right and left—for he goes it
   In earnest when once he's begun.
Descensus averni—he knows it;
   It's easy for "Gentleman, One."

The crash comes as sure as the seasons;
   He loses his coin in a mine,
Or booming in land, or for reasons
   Connected with women and wine.
Or maybe the cards or the horses
   A share of the damage have done.
No matter; the end of the course is
   The same: "*Re* a Gentleman, One."

He struggles a while to keep going,
   To stave off detection and shame;
But creditors clamorous growing
   Ere long put an end to the game.
At length the poor soldier of Satan
   His course to a finish has run—
And just think of Windeyer waiting
   To deal with "a Gentleman, One!"

And some face it boldly, and brazen
   The shame and the utter disgrace;
While others, more sensitive, hasten
   Their names and their deeds to efface.
They snap the frail thread which the Furies
   And Fates have so cruelly spun.
May the Great Final Judge and His juries
   Have mercy on "Gentleman, One!"

THE TRAVELLING POST OFFICE

MARCH 1894

The roving breezes come and go, the reed beds sweep and sway,
The sleep river murmurs low, and loiters on its way,
It is the land of lots o' time along the Castlereagh.

The old man's son had left the farm, he found it dull and slow,
He drifted to the great North-west where all the rovers go.
"He's gone so long," the old man said, "he dropped right out of mind,
But if you'd write a line to him I'd take it very kind;
He's shearing here and fencing there, a kind of waif and stray,
He's droving now with Conroy's sheep along the Castlereagh.
The sheep are travelling for the grass, and travelling very slow;
They may be at Mundooran now, or past the Overflow,
Or tramping down the black soil flats across by Waddiwong,
But all those little country towns would send the letter wrong,
The mailman, if he's extra tired, would pass them in his sleep,
It's safest to address the note to 'Care of Conroy's sheep',
For five and twenty thousand head can scarcely go astray,
You write to 'Care of Conroy's sheep along the Castlereagh'."

By rock and ridge and riverside the western mail has gone,
Across the great Blue Mountain Range to take that letter on.
A moment on the topmost grade while open fire doors glare,
She pauses like a living thing to breathe the mountain air,
Then launches down the other side across the plains away
To bear that note to "Conroy's sheep along the Castlereagh".

And now by coach and mailman's bag it goes from town to town,
And Conroy's Gap and Conroy's Creek have marked it "further down".
Beneath a sky of deepest blue where never cloud abides,
A speck upon the waste of plain the lonely mailman rides.
Where fierce hot winds have set the pine and myall boughs asweep
He hails the shearers passing by for news of Conroy's sheep.
By big lagoons where wildfowl play and crested pigeons flock,
By campfires where the drovers ride around their restless stock,
And past the teamster toiling down to fetch the wool away
My letter chases Conroy's sheep along the Castlereagh.

BANJO PATERSON'S AUSTRALIANS

BANJO PATERSON'S AUSTRALIANS

THE OLD STATION

from *AN OUTBACK MARRIAGE*

There are few countries in the world with such varieties of climate as Australia, and though some stations are out in the great, red-hot, frying wastes of the Never-Never, others are up in the hills where a hot night is a thing unknown, where snow falls occasionally, and where it is no uncommon thing to spend a summer's evening by the side of a roaring fire. In the matter of improvements, too, stations vary greatly. Some are in a wilderness with fittings to match; others have telephones between homestead and out-stations, the jackeroos dress for dinner, and the station hands are cowed into touching their hats and saying "Sir". Also stations are of all sizes, and the man who is considered quite a big squatter in the settled districts is thought small potatoes by the magnate "out back", who shears a hundrd and fifty thousand sheep, and has an overdraft like the National Debt.

Kuryong was a hill-country station of about sixty thousand acres all told; but they were good acres, as no one knew better than old Bully Grant, the owner, of whose history and disposition we heard something from Pinnock at the club. It was a highly improved place, with a fine homestead— thanks to Bully Grant's money, for in the old days it had been a very different sort of place— and its history is typical of hundreds of others.

When Andrew Gordon first bought it, it was held under lease from the Crown, and there were no improvements to speak of. The station homestead, so lovingly descanted upon in the advertisement consisted of a two-roomed slab hut; the woolshed, where the sheep were shorn, was made of gumtree trunks roofed with bark. The wool went down to Sydney, and station supplies came back, in huge waggons drawn by eighteen or twenty bullocks, that travelled nine miles a day on a journey of three hundred miles. There were no neighbours except at the township of Kiley's Crossing, which consisted of two public-houses and a store. It was a rough life for the young squatter, and evidently he found it lonely; for on a visit to Sydney he fell in love with and married a dainty girl of French descent. Refined, well-educated, and fragile-looking, she seemed about the last person in the world to take out to a slab-hut homestead as a squatter's wife. But there is an old saying that blood will tell; and with all the courage of her Huguenot ancestry she faced the roughness and discomforts of bush life. On her arrival at the station the old two-roomed hut was plastered and whitewashed, additional rooms were built, and quite a neat little home was the result. Seasons were good, and the young squatter might have gone on shearing sheep and selling fat stock till the end of his life but for the advent of free selection in 1861.

In that year the Legislature threw open all leasehold lands to the public for purchase on easy terms and conditions. The idea was to settle an industrious peasantry on lands hitherto leased in large blocks to the squatters. This brought down a flood of settlement on Kuryong. At the top end of the station there was a chain of mountains, and the country was rugged and patchy—

rich valleys alternating with ragged hills. Here and there about the run were little patches of specially good land, which were soon snapped up. The pioneers of these small settlers were old Morgan Donohoe and his wife, who had built the hotel at Kiley's Crossing; and, on their reports, all their friends and relatives, as they came out of the "ould country", worked their way to Kuryong, and built little bits of slab and bark homesteads in among the mountains. The rougher the country, the better they liked it. They were a horse-thieving, sheep-stealing breed, and the talents which made them poachers in the old country soon made them champion bushmen in their new surroundings. The leader of these mountain settlers was one Doyle, a gigantic Irishman, who had got a grant of a few hundred acres in the mountains, and had taken to himself a Scotch wife from among the free immigrants. The story ran that he was too busy to go to town, but asked a friend to go and pick a wife for him "a fine shtrappin' woman, wid a good brisket on her".

The Doyles were large, slow, heavy men, with an instinct for the management of cattle; they were easily distinguished from the Donohoes, who were little red-whiskered men, enterprising and quick-witted, and ready to do anything in the world for a good horse. Other strangers and outlanders came to settle in the district, but from the original settlement up to the date of our story the two great families of the Doyles and the Donohoes governed the neighbourhood, and the headquarters of the clans was at Donohoe's "Shamrock Hotel", at Kiley's Crossing. Here they used to *rendezvous* when they went away down to the plains country each year for the shearing; for they added to their resources by travelling about the country shearing, droving, fencing, tanksinking, or doing any other job that offered itself, but always returned to their mountain fastnesses ready for any bit of work "on the cross" (i.e., unlawful) that might turn up. When times got hard they had a handy knack of finding horses that nobody had lost, shearing sheep they did not own and branding and selling other people's calves.

When they stole stock, they moved them on through the mountains as quickly as possible, always having a brother or uncle, or a cousin—Terry or Timothy or Martin or Patsy—who had a holding "beyant". By these means they could shift stolen stock across the great range, and dispose of them among the peaceable folk who dwelt in the good country on the other side, whose stock they stole in return. Many a good horse and fat beast had made the stealthy mountain journey, lying hidden in gaps and gullies when pursuit grew hot, and being moved on as things quieted down.

Another striking feature was the way in which they got themselves mixed up with each other. Their names were so tangled up that no one could keep tally of them. There was a Red Mick Donohoe (son of the old publican), and his cousin Black Mick Donohoe, and Red Mick's son Mick, and Black Mick's son Mick, and Red Mick's son Pat, and Black Mick's son Pat; and there

BANJO PATERSON'S AUSTRALIANS

was Gammy Doyle (meaning Doyle with the lame leg), and Scrammy Doyle (meaning Doyle with the injured arm), Bosthoon Doyle and Omadhaun Doyle—a Bosthoon being a man who never had any great amount of sense to speak of, while an Omadhaun is a man who began life with some sense, but lost most of it on his journey. It was a common saying in the country-side that if you met a man on the mountains you should say, "Good day, Doyle," and if he replied, "That's not my name," you should at once say, "Well, I meant no offence, Mr Donohoe."

One could generally pick which was which of the original stock, but when they came to intermarry there was no telling t'other from which. Startling likenesses cropped up among the relatives, and it was widely rumoured that one Doyle who was known to be in gaol, and who was vaguely spoken of by the clan as being "away", was in fact serving an accumulation of sentences for himself and other members of the family, whose sins he had for a consideration taken on himself.

With such neighbours as these fighting him for every block of land, Andrew Gordon soon came to the end of his resources, and it was then that he had to take in his old manager as a partner. Before Bully Grant had been in the firm long, he had secured nearly all the good land, and the industrious yeomanry that the Land Act was supposed to create were hiding away up the gullies on miserable little patches of bad land, stealing sheep for a living. Bully fought them stoutly, impounded their sheep and cattle, and prosecuted trespassers and thieves; and, his luck being wonderful, he soon added to the enormous fortune he had made in mining, while Andrew Gordon died impoverished. When he died, old Bully gave the management of the stations to his sons, and contented himself with finding fault. But one dimly remembered episode in his career was talked of by the old hands around Kiley's Hotel, long after Grant had become a wealthy man, and had gone for long trips to England.

Grant, in spite of the judgment and sagacity on which he prided himself, had at various times in his career made mistakes—mistakes in station management, mistakes about stock, mistakes about men, and last, but now least, mistakes about women; and it was to one of these mistakes that the gossips referred.

When he was a young man working as Mr Gordon's manager, and living with the horse-breaker and the ration-carrier on the out-station at Kuryong (in those days a wild, half-civilised place), he had for neighbours Red Mick's father and mother, the original Mr and Mrs Donohoe, and their family. Their eldest daughter, Peggy—"Carrotty Peg", her relations called her—was at that time a fine, strapping, bush girl, and the only unmarried white woman anywhere near the station. She was as fair-complexioned as Red Mick himself, with a magnificent head of red hair, and the bust and limbs of a young Amazon.

This young woman, as she grew up, attracted the attention of Billy the Bully, and they used

BANJO PATERSON'S AUSTRALIANS

to meet a good deal out in the bush. On such occasions, he would possibly be occupied in the inspiriting task of dragging a dead sheep after his horse, to make a trail to lead the wild dogs up to some poisoned meat; while the lady, clad in light and airy garments, with a huge white sunbonnet for head-gear, would be riding straddle-legged in search of strayed cows. When Grant left the station, and went away to make his fortune in mining, it was, perhaps, just a coincidence that this magnificent young creature grew tired of the old place and "cleared out", too. She certainly went away and disappeared so utterly that even her own people did not know what had become of her; to the younger generation her very existence was only a vague tradition. But it was whispered here and muttered there among the Doyles and the Donohoes and their friends and relations, that old Billy the Bully, on one of his visits to the interior, had been married to this undesirable lady by a duly accredited parson, in the presence of responsible witnesses; and that, when everyone had their own, Carrotty Peg, if alive, would be the lady of Kuryong. However, she had never come back to prove it, and no one cared about asking her alleged husband any unpleasant questions.

So much for the history of its owners; now to describe the homestead itself. It had originally consisted of the two-roomed slab hut, which had been added to from time to time. Kitchen, outhouses, bachelors' quarters, saddle-rooms, and store-rooms had been built on in a kind of straggling quadrangle, with many corners and unexpected doorways and passages; and it is reported that a swagman once got his dole of rations at the kitchen, went away, and after turning two or three corners, got so tangled up that when Fate led him back to the kitchen he didn't recognise it, and asked for the rations over again, in the firm belief that he was at a different part of the house.

The original building was still the principal living-room, but the house had grown till it contained about twenty rooms. The slab walls had been plastered and whitewashed, and a wide verandah ran all along the front. Round the house were acres of garden, with great clumps of willows and acacias, where the magpies sat in the heat of the day and sang to one another in their sweet, low warble.

The house stood on a spur running from the hills. Looking down the river from it, one saw level flats waving with long grasses, in which the solemn cattle waded knee-deep. Here and there clumps of willows and stately poplars waved in the breeze. In the clear, dry air all colours were startlingly vivid, and round the nearer foothills wonderful lights and shadows played and shifted, while sometimes a white fleece of mist would drift slowly across a distant hill, like a film of snowy lace on the face of a beautiful woman. Away behind the foothills were the grand old mountains, with their snow-clad tops gleaming in the sun.

The garden was almost as lacking in design as the house. There were acres of fruit trees, with prairie grass growing at their roots, trees whereon grew luscious peaches and juicy egg-plums; long vistas of grapevines, with little turnings and alleys, regular lovers' walks, where the scent of honeysuckle intoxicated the senses. At the foot of the garden was the river, a beautiful stream, fed by the mountain-snow, and rushing joyously over clear gravel beds, whose million-tinted pebbles flashed in the sunlight like so many opals.

In some parts of Australia it is difficult to tell summer from winter; but up in this mountain-country each season had its own attractions. In the spring the flats were green with lush grass, speckled with buttercups and bachelors' buttons, and the willows put out their new leaves, and all manner of shy dry-scented bush flowers bloomed on the ranges; and the air was full of the song of birds and the calling of animals. Then came summer, when never a cloud decked the arch of blue sky, and all animated nature drew into the shade of big trees until the evening breeze sprang up, bringing sweet scents of the dry grass and ripening grain. In autumn, the leaves of the English trees turned all tints of yellow and crimson, and the grass in the paddocks went brown; and the big bullock teams worked from dawn till dark, hauling in their loads of hay from the cultivation paddocks.

But most beautiful of all was winter, when logs blazed in the huge fireplaces, and frosts made the ground crisp, and the stock, long-haired and shaggy, came snuffling round the stables, picking up odds and ends of straw; when the grey, snow-clad mountains looked but a stone's throw away in the intensely clear air, and the wind brought a colour to the cheeks and a tingling to the blood that made life worth living.

Such was Kuryong homestead, where lived Charlie Gordon's mother and his brother Hugh, with a lot of children left by another brother who, like many others, had gone up to Queensland to make his fortune, and had left his bones there instead; and to look after these young folk there was a governess, Miss Harriott.

THE OLD AUSTRALIAN WAYS

1902

The London lights are far abeam
  Behind a bank of cloud,
Along the shore the gas lights gleam,
  The gale is piping loud;
And down the Channel, groping blind,
  We drive her through the haze
Towards the land we left behind—
The good old land of "never mind",
  And old Australian ways.

The narrow ways of English folk
  Are not for such as we;
They bear the long-accustomed yoke
  Of staid conservancy:
But all our roads are new and strange
  And through our blood there runs
The vagabonding love of change
That drove us westward of the range
  And westward of the suns.

The city folk go to and fro
  Behind a prison's bars,
They never feel the breezes blow
  And never see the stars;
They never hear in blossomed trees
  The music low and sweet
Of wild birds making melodies,
Nor catch the little laughing breeze
  That whispers in the wheat.

Our fathers came of roving stock
  That could not fixed abide:
And we have followed field and flock
  Since e'er we learnt to ride;
By miner's camp and shearing shed,
  In land of heat and drought,
We followed where our fortunes led,
With fortune always on ahead
  And always further out.

The wind is in the barley grass,
  The wattles are in bloom;
The breezes greet us as they pass
  With honey-sweet perfume;
The parakeets go screaming by
  With flash of golden wing,
And from the swamp the wild ducks cry
Their long-drawn note of revelry,
  Rejoicing at the spring.

So throw the weary pen aside
  And let the papers rest,
For we must saddle up and ride
  Towards the blue hill's breast;
And we must travel far and fast
  Across their rugged maze,
To find the Spring of Youth at last,
And call back from the buried past
  The old Australian ways.

When Clancy took the drover's track
  In years of long ago,
He drifted to the outer back
  Beyond the Overflow;
By rolling plain and rocky shelf,
  With stockwhip in his hand,
He reached at last, oh lucky elf,
The Town of Come-and-Help-Yourself
  In Rough-and-Ready Land.

And if it be that you would know
  The tracks he used to ride,
Then you must saddle up and go
  Beyond the Queensland side—
Beyond the reach of rule or law,
  To ride the long day through,
In Nature's homestead—filled with awe:
You then might see what Clancy saw
  And know what Clancy knew.

BANJO PATERSON'S AUSTRALIANS

THE GREAT CALAMITY

AUGUST 1893

MacFierce'un came to Whiskeyhurst
  When summer days were hot,
And bided there wi' Jock McThirst,
  A brawny brother Scot.
Gude Faith! They made the whisky fly,
  Like Highland chieftains true,
And when they'd drunk the beaker dry
  They sang, "We are nae fou!"

"There is nae folk like oor ain folk,
  Sae gallant and sae true."
They sang the only Scottish joke
  Which is, "We are nae fou."

Said bold McThirst, "Let Saxons jaw
  Aboot their great concerns,
But bonny Scotland beats them a',
  The land o' cakes and Burns,
The land o' partridge, deer, and grouse,
  Fill up your glass, I beg,
There's muckle whusky i' the house,
  Forbye what's in the keg."

And here a hearty laugh he laughed,
  "Just come wi' me, I beg."
MacFierce'un saw with pleasure daft
  A fifty-gallon keg.

"Losh, man, that's grand," MacFierc'un cried,
  "Saw ever man the like?
Now, wi' the daylight, I maun ride
  To meet a Southron tyke,
But I'll be back ere summer's gone,
  So bide for me, I beg,
We'll make a grand assault upon
  Yon deevil of a keg."

       * * * *

MacFierce'un rode to Whiskeyhurst,
  When summer days were gone,
And there he met with Jock McThirst
  Was greetin' all alone.

"McThirst, what gars ye look sae blank?
  Have all yer wits gane daft?
Has that accursed Southron bank
  Called up your overdraft?

"Is all your grass burnt up wi' drouth?
  Is wool and hides gone flat?"
McThirst replied, "Gude friend, in truth,
  'Tis muckle waur than that.

"Has sair misfortune cursed your life
  That you should weep sae free?
Is harm upon your bonny wife,
  The children at your knee?
Is scaith upon your house and hame?"
  McThirst upraised his head:
"My bairns hae done the deed of shame—
  'Twere better they were dead.

"To think my bonny infant son
  Should do the deed o' guilt—
He let the whuskey spigot run,
  And a' the whuskey's spilt!"

       * * * *

Upon them both these words did bring
  A solemn silence deep,
Gude faith, it is a fearsome thing
  To see two strong men weep.

THE MAN FROM IRONBARK

DECEMBER 1892

It was the man from Ironbark who struck the Sydney town,
He wandered over street and park, he wandered up and down.
He loitered here, he loitered there, till he was like to drop,
Until at last in sheer despair he sought a barber's shop.
"'Ere! shave my beard and whiskers off, I'll be a man of mark,
I'll go and do the Sydney toff up home in Ironbark."

The barber man was small and flash, as barbers mostly are,
He wore a strike-your-fancy sash, he smoked a huge cigar;
He was a humorist of note and keen at repartee,
He laid the odds and kept a "tote", whatever that may be,
And when he saw our friend arrive, he whispered, "Here's a lark!
Just watch me catch him all alive, this man from Ironbark."

There were some gilded youths that sat along the barber's wall.
Their eyes were dull, their heads were flat, they had no brains at all;
To them the barber passed the wink, his dexter eyelid shut,
"I'll make this bloomin' yokel think his bloomin' throat is cut."
And as he soaped and rubbed it in he made a rude remark:
"I s'pose the flats is pretty green up there in Ironbark."

A grunt was all reply he got; he shaved the bushman's chin,
Then made the water boiling hot and dipped the razor in.
He raised his hand, his brow grew black, he paused awhile to gloat,
Then slashed the red-hot razor-back across his victim's throat;
Upon the newly-shaven skin it made a livid mark—
No doubt it fairly took him in—the man from Ironbark.

He fetched a wild up-country yell might wake the dead to hear,
And though his throat, he knew full well, was cut from ear to ear,
He struggled gamely to his feet, and faced the murd'rous foe:
"You've done for me! you dog, I'm beat! one hit before I go!
I only wish I had a knife, you blessed murdering shark!
But you'll remember all your life the man from Ironbark."

He lifted up his hairy paw, with one tremendous clout
He landed on the barber's jaw, and knocked the barber out.
He set to work with nail and tooth, he made the place a wreck;
He grabbed the nearest gilded youth, and tried to break his neck.
And all the while his throat he held to save his vital spark,
And "Murder! Bloody murder!" yelled the man from Ironbark.

A peeler man who heard the din came in to see the show;
He tried to run the bushman in, but he refused to go.
And when at last the barber spoke, and said " 'Twas all in fun—
'Twas just a little harmless joke, a trifle overdone."
"A joke!" he cried, "By George, that's fine; a lively sort of lark;
I'd like to catch that murdering swine some night in Ironbark."

And now while round the shearing floor the list'ning shearers gape,
He tells the story o'er and o'er, and brags of his escape.
"Them barber chaps what keeps a tote, By George, I've had enough,
One tried to cut my bloomin' throat, but thank the Lord it's tough."
And whether he's believed or no, there's one thing to remark,
That flowing beards are all the go way up in Ironbark.

Hay and Hell and Booligal

APRIL 1896

"You come and see me, boys," he said;
"You'll find a welcome and a bed
   And whisky any time you call;
Although our township hasn't got
The name of quite a lively spot—
   You see, I live in Booligal.

"And people have an awful down
Upon the district and the town—
   Which worse than hell itself they call;
In fact, the saying far and wide
Along the Riverina side
   Is 'Hay and Hell and Booligal'.

"No doubt it suits 'em very well
To say it's worse than Hay or Hell,
   But don't you heed their talk at all;
Of course, there's heat—no one denies—
And sand and dust and stacks of flies,
   And rabbits, too, at Booligal.

"But such a pleasant, quiet place,
You never see a stranger's face—
   They hardly ever care to call;
The drovers mostly pass it by;
They reckon that they'd rather die
   Than spend a night in Booligal.

"The big mosquitoes frighten some—
You'll lie awake to hear 'em hum—
   And snakes about the township crawl;

But shearers, when they get their cheque,
They never come along and wreck
   The blessed town of Booligal.

"But down in Hay the shearers come
And fill themselves with fighting rum,
   And chase blue devils up the wall,
And fight the snaggers every day,
Until there is the deuce to pay—
   There's none of that in Booligal.

"Of course, there isn't much to see—
The billiard table use to be
   The great attraction for us all,
Until some careless, drunken curs
Got sleeping on it in their spurs,
   And ruined it, in Booligal.

"Just now there is a howling drought
That pretty near has starved us out—
   It never seems to rain at all;
But, if there *should* come any rain,
You couldn't cross the black soil plain—
   You'd have to stop in Booligal."

"*We'd have to stop!*" With bated breath
We prayed that both in life and death
   Our fate in other lines might fall:
"Oh, send us to our just reward
In Hay or Hell, but, gracious Lord,
   Deliver us from Booligal!"

SITTING IN JUDGMENT

A SHOW RING SKETCH

The scene is an Australian country show ring—a circular enclosure of about four acres extent—with a spiked batten fence round it, and a listless crowd of back-country settlers hanging around the fence. Back of these there are the sheds for produce, and the machinery sections, where steam threshers and earth scoops are humming, and buzzing, and thundering unnoticed. Crowds of sightseers wander along the cattle stalls and gape at the fat bullocks; side shows are flourishing, a blasé goose is drawing marbles out of a tin canister, and a boxing showman is showing his muscles outside his tent while his partner urges the youth of the district to come in and be thumped for the edification of the audience.

Suddenly a gate opens at the end of the show ring, and horses, cattle, dogs, vehicles, motor cars, and bicyclists crowd into the arena. It is called a general parade, but it might better be described as general chaos.

Trotting horses and ponies, in harness, go whirling round the ring, every horse and every driver fully certain that every eye is fixed on them; the horses—the vainest creatures in the world—arch their necks, and lift their feet up, whizzing past in bewildering succesion, till the onlookers get giddy at the constant thud, thud, thud of the hoofs and the rustle of the wheels.

Inside the whirling circle of vehicles, blood stallions are standing on their hind legs, and screaming defiance at all comers; great shaggy-fronted bulls, with dull vindictive eyes, pace along, looking as though they were trying to remember who it was that struck them last. A showground bull always seems to be nursing a grievance.

Mixed up with the stallions and bulls are dogs and donkeys, the dogs being led by attendants, who are apparently selected on the principle that the larger the dog, the smaller the custodian should be, while the donkeys are the only creatures absolutely unmoved by their surroundings, for they sleep peaceably as they walk along, occasionally waking up to utter melodious hoots.

In the centre of the ring a few lady riders, stern-featured women for the most part, are being "judged" by a trembling official, who dares not look any of them in the face, but hurriedly and apologetically examines the horses and saddles, whispers his award to the stewards, and runs at top speed to the official stand, which he reaches in safety just as the award is made known to the competitors.

The defeated ladies immediately begin to "perform" i.e., to ask the universe at large whether anyone ever heard the like of that! But the stewards slip away like shadows, and they are left "performing" to empty benches, so they ride haughtily round the ring, glaring defiance at the spectators.

All the time that the parade is going on, stewards and committee men are wandering about among the competitors trying to find the animals to be judged. The clerk of the ring—a huge man mounted on a small cob—gallops about, roaring out in a voice like a bull: "This way for the fourteen-stone 'acks! Come on, you twelve-'and ponies!" and by degrees various classes get judged, and disperse grumbling. Then the bulls begin to file out with their grievances still unsettled, the lady riders are persuaded to withdraw, and the clerk of the ring sends a sonorous bellow across the ground: "Where's the jumpin' judges?"

From the official stand comes a brisk, dark-faced, wiry little man; he has been a steeple-chase rider and a trainer in his time; long experience of that tricky animal, the horse, has made him reserved and slow to express an opinion; he mounts the table, and produces a notebook; from the bar of the booth comes a large, hairy, red-faced man, a man whose face shows absolute self-content. He is a noted show judge, because he refuses, as a rule, to listen to anybody else's opinion, and when he does listen to it, he scornfully contradicts it, as a matter of course. The third judge is a local squatter, who has never judged before, and is overwhelmed with a sense of his own importance.

They seat themselves on a raised platform in the centre of the ring, and hold consultation. The small dark man produces his notebook.

"I always keep a scale of points," he says. "Give 'em so many points for each fence. Then give 'em so many for make, shape, and quality, and so many for the way they jump."

The fat man looks infinite contempt. "I never want any scale of points," he says. "One look at the 'orses is enough for me. A man that judges by points ain't a judge at all, I reckon. What do you think?" he goes on, turning to the squatter. "Do you use points?"

"Never," says the squatter, firmly; which as he has never judged before in his life, is not at all surprising.

"Well, we'll each go our own way," says the little man. "I'll keep points. Send 'em in."

"Number one: Conductor!" roars the ring steward in a voice like thunder, and a long-legged grey horse comes trotting into the ring and sidles about uneasily. His rider points him for the first jump, and goes at it at a terrific pace. Nearing the fence the horse makes a wild spring, and clears it by feet, while the crowd yell applause; at the second jump he races right close under the obstacle, props dead, and rises in the air with a leap like a goat, while the crowd yell their delight again, and say, "My oath! Ain't he clever?" At the third fence he shifts about uneasily as he comes near it and finally darts at it at an angle, clearing about thirty feet quite unnecessarily, and again the hurricane of cheers breaks out. "Don't he fly 'em?" says one man, waving his hat. At the last fence he makes his spring yards too soon, and, while his forelegs get over all right, his hind legs drop on the rail with a sounding rap, and he leaves a little tuft of hair sticking in the fence.

"I like to see 'em feel their fences," says the fat man. "I had a bay 'orse once, and he felt every fence ever he jumped; shows their confidence."

"I think he'll feel that last one for awhile," says the little dark man. "He hit it pretty hard. What's this now?"

"Number two: Homeward Bound!" And an old solid chestnut horse comes out, and canters up to each jump, clearing them coolly and methodically, always making his spring at the correct distance from the fence. The crowd are not struck by the performance, and the fat man says, "No pace!" but surreptitiously makes two strokes to indicate number two on the cuff of his shirt.

"Number eleven: Spite!" A leggy, weedy chestnut brute, half racehorse, half nondescript, ridden by a terrified amateur, who goes at the fence with a white set face. The horse races up to the fence, and stops dead, among the jeers of the crowd. The rider lets daylight into him with him spurs, and rushes him at the fence again, and this time he gets over.

Round he goes, clouting some fences with his front legs, others with his hind legs. The crowd jeer, but the fat man, from a sheer spirit of opposition, says, "That would be a good horse if he was rode better." And the squatter says, "Yes, he belongs to a young feller just near me. I've seen him jump splendidly out in the bush, over brush fences."

The little dark man says nothing, but makes a note in his book.

"Number twelve: Gaslight!" "Now, you'll see a horse," says the fat man. "I've judged this 'orse in twenty different shows, and gave him first prize every time!"

Gaslight turns out to be a fiddle-headed, heavy-shouldered brute, whose long experience of jumping in shows where they give points for pace, as if the affair were a steeplechase, has taught him to get the business over as quickly as he can. He goes thundering round the ring, pulling double, and standing off his fences in a style that would infallibly bring him to grief if following hounds across roads or through broken timber.

"Now," says the fat man, "that's a 'unter, that is. What I say is, when you come to judge at a show, pick out the 'orse that you would soonest be on if Ned Kelly was after you, and there you have the best 'unter." The little man makes no reply, but makes his usual scrawl in the book, while the squatter hastens to agree with the fat man. "I like to see a bit of pace myself," he ventures to remark.

The fat man sits on him heavily. "You don't call that pace, do you?" he says. "He was only going dead slow."

Various other competitors come in and do their turn round the ring, come propping and bucking over the jumps, others rushing and tearing at their fences, none jumping as a hunter ought to do. Some get themselves into difficulties by changing their feet or misjudging their distance, and

are loudly applauded by the crowd for their "cleverness" in getting themselves out of difficulties which, if they had any cleverness, they would not have got into.

A couple of rounds narrow the competitors down to a few, and the task of deciding is then entered upon.

"I have kept a record," says the little man, "of how they jump each fence, and I give them points for style of jumping, and for their make and shape and hunting qualities. The way I bring it out is that Homeward Bound is the best, with Gaslight second."

"Homeward Bound!" says the fat man. "Why, the pace he went wouldn't head a duck. He didn't go as fast as a Chinaman could trot with two baskets of stones. I want to have three of 'em in to have a look at 'em." Here he looks surreptitiously at his cuff, and seeing a note, "No. II," mistakes it for "number eleven," and says: "I want number eleven to go another round."

This order is shouted across the ground, and the leggy, weedy chestnut with the terrified amateur up, comes sidling and snorting out into the ring. The fat man looks at him with scorn.

"What is that fiddle-headed brute doing in the ring?" he says.

"Why," says the ring steward, "you said you wanted him."

"Well," says the fat man, "if I wanted him, I *do* want him. Let him go the round."

The terrified amateur goes at the fences with the rashness of despair, and narrowly escapes being clouted off on two occasions. This puts the fat man in a quandary, because, as he has kept no record, he has got all the horses jumbled up in his head, but he has one fixed idea, viz., to give first prize to Gaslight; as to what is to come second he is open to argument. From sheer contrariness he says that number eleven would be "all right if he were rode better", and the squatter agrees. The little man is overruled, and the prizes go—Gaslight, first; Spite, second; Homeward Bound, third.

The crowd hoot loudly as Spite's rider comes round with the second ribbon, and the small boys suggest to the judge in shrill tones that he ought to boil his head. The fat man stalks majestically into the steward's stand, and on being asked how he came to give Spite the second prized, remarks oracularly: "I judge the 'orse; I don't judge the rider."

This silences criticism, and everyone adjourns to have a drink.

Over the flowing bowl the fat man says, "You see, I don't believe in this nonsense about points. I can judge 'em without that."

The scene closes with twenty dissatisfied competitors riding away from the ring, vowing they will never bring another horse there in their lives, and one, the winner, saying: "Bly me, I knew it would be all right with old Billy judging. 'E *knows* this 'orse."

FATHER RILEY'S HORSE

DECEMBER 1899

'Twas the horse thief, Andy Regan, that was hunted like a dog
　By the troopers of the upper Murray side,
They had searched in every gully—they had looked in every log,
　But never sight or track of him they spied,
Till the priest at Kiley's Crossing heard a knocking very late
　And a whisper "Father Riley—come across!"
So his Rev'rence in pyjamas trotted softly to the gate
　And admitted Andy Regan—and a horse!

"Now, it's listen, Father Riley, to the words I've got to say,
　For it's close upon my death I am tonight.
With the troopers hard behind me I've been hiding all the day
　In the gullies keeping close and out of sight.
But they're watching all the ranges till there's not a bird could fly,
　And I'm fairly worn to pieces with the strife,
So I'm taking no more trouble, but I'm going home to die,
　'Tis the only way I see to save my life.

"Yes, I'm making home to mother's, and I'll die o' Tuesday next
　An' be buried on the Thursday—and, of course,
I'm prepared to meet my penance, but with one thing I'm perplexed
　And it's—Father, it's this jewel of a horse!
He was never bought nor paid for, and there's not a man can swear
　To his owner or his breeder, but I know,
That his sire was by Pedantic from the Old Pretender mare
　And his dam was close related to The Roe.

"And there's nothing in the district that can race him for a step,
　He could canter while they're going at their top:
He's the king of all the leppers that was ever seen to lep,
　A five-foot fence—he'd clear it in a hop!
So I'll leave him with you, Father, till the dead shall rise again,
　'Tis yourself that knows a good 'un; and, of course,
You can say he's got by Moonlight out of Paddy Murphy's plain
　If you're ever asked the breeding of the horse!

"But it's getting on to daylight and it's time to say goodbye,
　For the stars above the east are growing pale.
And I'm making home to mother—and it's hard for me to die!
　But it's harder still, is keeping out of gaol!
You can ride the old horse over to my grave across the dip
　Where the wattle bloom is waving overhead.
Sure he'll jump them fences easy—you must never raise the whip
　Or he'll rush 'em—now, goodbye!" and he had fled!

So they buried Andy Regan, and they buried him to rights,
　In the graveyard a the back of Kiley's Hill;
There were five-and-twenty mourners who had five-and-twenty fights
　Till the very boldest fighters had their fill.
There were fifty horses racing from the graveyard to the pub,
　And their riders flogged each other all the while.
And the lashin's of the liquor! And the lavin's of the grub!
　Oh, poor Andy went to rest in proper style.

Then the races came to Kiley's—with a steeplechase and all,
　For the folk were mostly Irish round about,
And it takes an Irish rider to be fearless of a fall,
　They were training morning in and morning out.
But they never started training till the sun was on the course
　For a superstitious story kept 'em back,
That the ghost of Andy Regan on a slashing chestnut horse,
　Had been training by the starlight on the track.

And they read the nominations for the races with surprise
　And amusement at the Father's little joke,
For a novice had been entered for the steeplechasing prize,
　And they found that it was Father Riley's moke!
He was neat enough to gallop, he was strong enough to stay!
　But his owner's views of training were immense,
For the Reverend Father Riley used to ride him every day,
　And he never saw a hurdle nor a fence.

And the priest would join the laughter: "Oh," said he, "I put him in,
  For there's five-and-twenty sovereigns to be won.
And the poor would find it useful, if the chestnut chanced to win,
  And he'll maybe win when all is said and done!"
He had called him Faugh-a-ballagh, which is French for "clear the course",
  And his colours were a vivid shade of green:
All the Dooleys and O'Donnells were on Father Riley's horse,
  While the Orangemen were backing Mandarin!

It was Hogan, the dog poisoner—aged man and very wise,
  Who was camping in the racecourse with his swag,
And who ventured the opinion, to the township's great surprise,
  That the race would go to Father Riley's nag.
"You can talk about your riders—and the horse has not been schooled,
  And the fences is terrific, and the rest!
When the field is fairly going, then ye'll see ye've all been fooled,
  And the chestnut horse will battle with the best.

"For there's some has got condition, and they think the race is sure,
  And the chestnut horse will fall beneath the weight,
But the hopes of all the helpless, and the prayers of all the poor,
  Will be running by his side to keep him straight.
And it's what's the need of schoolin' or of workin' on the track,
  Whin the saints are there to guide him round the course!
I've prayed him over every fence—I've prayed him out and back!
  And I'll bet my cash on Father Riley's horse!"

Oh, the steeple was a caution! They went tearin' round and round,
  And the fences rang and rattled where they struck.
There was some that cleared the water—there was more fell in and drowned,
  Some blamed the men and others blamed the luck!
But the whips were flying freely when the field came into view,
  For the finish down the long green stretch of course,
And in front of all the flyers—jumpin' like a kangaroo,
  Came the rank outsider—Father Riley's horse!

Oh, the shouting and the cheering as he rattled past the post!
  For he left the others standing, in the straight;
And the rider—well they reckoned it was Andy Regan's ghost,
  And it beat 'em how a ghost would draw the weight!
But he weighed in, nine stone seven, then he laughed and disappeared,
  Like a banshee (which is Spanish for an elf),
And old Hogan muttered sagely, "If it wasn't for the beard
  They'd be thinking it was Andy Regan's self!"

And the poor of Kiley's Crossing drank the health at Christmastide
  Of the chestnut and his rider dressed in green.
There was never such a rider, not since Andy Regan died,
  And they wondered who on earth he could have been.
But they settled it among 'em, for the story got about,
  'Mongst the bushmen and the people on the course,
That the Devil had been ordered to let Andy Regan out
  For the steeplechase on Father Riley's horse!

The Merino Sheep

DECEMBER 1895

The prosperity of Australia is absolutely based on a beast—the merino sheep. If all the sheep in the country were to die, the big banks would collapse like card houses, the squatting securities, which are their backbone, being gone. Business would perish, and the money we owe to England would be as hopelessly lost to that nation as if we were a South American state. The sheep, and the sheep alone, keeps us going. On the back of his beneficent creature we all live. Knowing this, people have got the impression that the merino sheep is a gentle, bleating animal that gets its living without trouble to anybody, and comes up every year to be shorn with a pleased smile upon its amiable face. It is my purpose here, as one having experience, to exhibit the merino sheep in its true light, so that the public may know what kind of brute they are depending on.

And first let us give him what little credit is his due. No one can accuse him of being a ferocious animal. No one could ever say that a sheep attacked him without provocation, though there is an old bush story of a man who was discovered in the act of killing a neighbour's whether. "Hullo,' said the neighbour. "What's this? Killing my sheep! What have you got to say for yourself?" "Yes," said the man, with an air of virtuous indignation. "I *am* killing your sheep. I'll kill *any* man's sheep that bites *me*!" But as a rule the merino refrains from using his teeth on people, and goes to work in another way.

The truth is that the merino sheep is a dangerous monomaniac, and his one idea is to ruin the man who owns him. With this object in view, he will display a talent for getting into trouble and a genius for dying that are almost incredible. If a mob of sheep see a bushfire closing round them, do they run away out of danger? Not at all; they rush round and round in a ring till the fire burns them up. If they are in a river bed, with a howling flood coming down, they will stubbornly refuse to cross three inches of water to save themselves. Dogs and men may bark and shriek, but the sheep won't move. They will wait there till the flood comes and drowns them all, and then their corpses go down the river on their backs with their feet in the air. A mob of sheep will crawl along a road slowly enough to exasperate a snail, but let a lamb get away from the mob in a bit of rough country, and a racehorse can't head him back again. If sheep are put into a big paddock with water in three corners of it, they will resolutely crowd into the fourth corner and die of thirst. When sheep are being counted out at a gate, if a scrap of bark be left on the ground in the gateway, they will refuse to step over it until dogs and men have sweated and toiled and sworn and "heeled 'em up", and "spoke to 'em", and fairly jammed them at it. Then the first one will gather courage, rush at the fancied obstacle, spring over it about six feet in the air and dart away. The next does exactly the same, but jumps a bit higher. Then comes a rush of them following one another in wild bounds like antelopes, until one "over-jumps himself" and alights on his head, a performance which nothing but a sheep could compass.

This frightens those still in the yard, and they stop running out, and the dogging and shrieking and hustling and tearing have to be gone through all over again. This on a red-hot day, mind you, with clouds of blinding dust about, with the yolk of wool irritating your eyes, and with, perhaps, three or four thousand sheep to put through. The delay throws out the man who is counting, and he forgets whether he left off at 45 or 95. The dogs, meanwhile, take the first chance to slip over the fence and hide in the shade somewhere. Then there are loud whistlings and oaths, and calls for Rover and Bluey, and at last a dirt-begrimed man jumps over the fence unearths a dog and hauls him back to work by the ear. The dog sets to barking and heeling 'em up again, and pretends that he thoroughly enjoys it, but he is looking out all the time for another chance to "clear". And *this* time he won't be discovered in a hurry.

To return to our muttons. There is a well-authenticated story of a shipload of sheep being lost once, because an old ram jumped overboard into the ocean, and all the rest followed him. No doubt they did, and were proud to do it. A sheep won't go through an open gate on his own responsibility, but he would gladly and proudly follow another sheep through the red-hot portals of Hades: and it makes no difference whether the leader goes voluntarily or is hauled struggling and kicking and fighting every inch of the way. For pure, sodden stupidity there is no animal like the merino sheep. A lamb will follow a bullock dray drawn by sixteen bullocks and driven by a profane "colonial" with a whip, under the impression that this aggregate monstrosity is his mother. A ewe never knows her own lamb by sight, and apparently has no sense of colour. She can recognise her own lamb's voice half a mile off among a thousand other voices apparently exactly similar, but when she gets within five yards of her lamb she starts to smell all the lambs in reach, including the black ones, though her own may be a white lamb. The fiendish resemblance which one sheep bears to another is a great advantage to them in their struggles with their owners. It makes them more difficult to draft out of a strange flock, and much harder to tell when any are missing.

Concerning this resemblance between sheep, there is a story told of a fat old Murrumbidgee squatter who gave a big price for a famous ram called, say, Sir Oliver. He took a friend out one day to inspect Sir Oliver, and overhauled that animal with a most impressive air of sheep wisdom. "Look here," he said, "at the fineness of the wool. See the serrations in each thread of it. See the density of it. Look at the way his legs and belly are clothed—he's wool all over, that sheep. Grand animal, grand animal!" Then they went and had a drink, and the old squatter said, "Now, I'll show you the difference between a champion ram and a second-rater". So he caught a ram and pointed out his defects. "See here—not half the serrations that other sheep had. No density of fleece to speak of. Bare-bellied as a pig, compared with Sir Oliver. Not that this isn't a fair sheep, but he'd be dear at one-tenth Sir Oliver's price. By the way, Johnson" (to his overseer) "what ram *is* this?" "That, sir" replied the astounded functionary, "that's Sir Oliver, sir!" And so it was.

There is another kind of sheep in Australia, as great a curse in his own way as the merino—

namely, the cross-bred or half-merino-half-Leicester animal. The cross-bred will get through, under or over any fence you like to put in front of him. He is never satisfied on his owner's run, but always thinks other people's runs must be better, so he sets off to explore. He will strike a course, say, south-east, and so long as the fit takes him he will keep going south-east through all obstacles, rivers, fences, growing crops—anything. The merino relies on passive resistance for his success; the cross-bred carries the war into the enemy's camp, and becomes a living curse to his owner day and night. Once there was a man who was induced in a weak moment to buy twenty cross-bred rams, and from that hour the hand of fate was upon him. They got into all the paddocks they shouldn't have been in. They scattered themselves all over the run promiscuously. They got into the cultivation paddock and the vegetable garden at their own sweet will. And then they took to roving. In a body they visited the neighbouring stations, and played havoc with the sheep all over the district. The wretched owner was constantly getting fiery letters from his neighbours: "Your . . . rams are here. Come and take them away at once", and he would have to go off nine or ten miles to drive them home. Any man who has to drive rams on a hot day knows what purgatory is. He was threatened with actions for trespass for scores of pounds damages every week. He tried shutting them up in the sheep yard. They got out and went back to the garden. Then he gaoled them in the calf pen. Out again and into a growing crop. Then he set a boy to watch them, but the boy went to sleep, and they were four miles away across country before he got on to their tracks. At length, when they happened accidentally to be at home on their owner's run, there came a huge flood. His sheep, mostly merinos, had plenty of time to get on to high ground and save their lives, but, of course, they didn't, and they were almost all drowned. The owner sat on a rise above the waste of waters and watched the dead animals go by. He was a ruined man. His hopes in life were gone. But he said, "Thank God, those rams are drowned, anyhow." Just as he spoke there was a splashing in the water, and the twenty rams solemnly swam ashore and ranged themselves in front of him. They were the only survivors of thousands of sheep. He broke down utterly, and was taken to an asylum for insane paupers. The cross-breds had fulfilled their destiny.

The cross-bred drives his owner out of his mind, but the merino ruins his man with greater celerity. Nothing on earth will kill cross-breds, while nothing will keep merinos alive. If they are put on dry saltbush country they die of drought. If they are put on damp, well-watered country they die of worms, fluke, and foot rot. They die in the wet seasons and they die in the dry ones. The hard, resentful look which you may notice on the faces of all bushmen comes from a long course of dealing with the merino sheep. It is the merino sheep which dominates the bush, and which gives to Australian literature its melancholy tinge, and its despairing pathos. The poems about dying boundary riders and lonely graves under mournful she-oaks are the direct outcome of the author's too close association with that soul-destroying animal, the merino sheep. A man who could write anything cheerful after a day in the drafting yards would be a freak of nature.

BANJO PATERSON'S AUSTRALIANS

THE MYLORA ELOPEMENT

DECEMBER 1886

By the winding Wollondilly where the weeping willows weep,
And the shepherd with his billy half awake and half asleep
Folds his fleecy flocks that linger homewards in the setting sun,
Lived my hero, Jim the Ringer, "cocky" on Mylora Run.

Jimmy loved the super's daughter, Miss Amelia Jane McGrath,
Long and earnestly he sought her, but he feared her stern papa;
And Amelia loved him truly—but the course of love, if true,
Never yet ran smooth or duly, as it ought, I think, to do.

Watching with his slow affection once Jim saw McGrath the boss
Riding out by Jim's selection, looking for a station 'oss
That was running in the ranges with a mob of outlaws wild,
Old McGrath "Good day" exchanges—off goes Jim to see his child;

Says, "The old man's after Stager, which he'll find is no light job,
And tomorrow I will wager he will try and yard the mob.
Will you come with me tomorrow, I will let the parson know,
And for ever joy, or sorrow, he will join us here below!

"I will bring my nags so speedy, Crazy Jane and Tambourine,
One more kiss—don't think I'm greedy—goodbye, lass, before I'm seen—
Just one more—God bless you, dearie! Don't forget to meet me here,
Life without you is but weary! now, once more goodbye, my dear."

    The daylight shines on figures twain
    That ride across Mylora plain,
    Laughing and talking—Jim and Jane.
    "Steadily, darling. There's lots of time,
    Didn't we slip the old man prime!
    I knew he'd tackle that Bowneck mob,
    I reckon he'll find it too big a job.
    They've beaten us all. I had a try,
    But the warrigal devils seem to fly.

That Sambo's a real good bit of stuff
No doubt, but not quite good enough.
He'll have to gallop the livelong day,
To cut and come, to race and stay.

I hope he yards 'em; 'twill do him good,
To see us going I don't think would."
A turn in the road, and fair and square,
They meet the old man standing there.
"What's up?" "Why, running away, of course,"
Says Jim, emboldened. The old man turned,
His eye with wild excitement burned.
"I've raced all day through the scorching heat
After old Bowneck: now I'm beat.
But over that range I think you'll find
The Bowneck mob all run stone-blind.
Will you go and leave the mob behind?
Which will you do? Take the girl away,
Or ride like a white man should today,
And yard old Bowneck? Go or stay?"
Says Jim, "I can't throw this away,
We can bolt some other day, of course,
Amelia Jane, get off that horse.
Up you get, old man. Whoop, halloo,
Here goes to put old Bowneck through!"
Two distant specks on the mountainside,
Two stockwhips echoing far and wide.
Amelia Jane sat down and cried.

"Sakes, Amelia, what's up now,
Leading old Sambo, too, I vow,
And him dead beat. Where have you been?
Bolted with Jim! What *do* you mean?
Met the old man with Sambo licked

From running old Bowneck. Well, I'm kicked.
Run 'em till Sambo nearly dropped?
What did Jim do when you were stopped?
Did you bolt from father across the plain?
Jim made you get off Crazy Jane!
And father got on, and away again.
The two of 'em went in the ranges grim.
Good boy, Jimmy! Well done, Jim!
They're sure to get them now, of course,
That Tambourine is a spanking horse.
And Crazy Jane is good as gold.
And Jim, they say, rides pretty bold;
Not like your father, but very fair.
Jim will have to follow the mare."
"It never was yet in father's hide
To best my Jim on the mountainside.
Jim can rally, and Jim can ride."
But here again Amelia cried.

The sound of a whip comes faint and far,
A rattle of hoofs, and here they are,
In all their tameless pride.
The fleet wild horses snort with fear,
And wheel and break as the yard draws near.
Now, Jim the Ringer, ride!
Wheel 'em! Wheel 'em! Wo back there, wo!
And the foam-flakes fly like the driven snow,

As under the whip the horses go
Adown the mountain side.

And Jim, hands down, and teeth firm set,
On a horse that never has failed him yet,
Is after them down the range.
Well ridden, well ridden, they wheel, wo back,
And long and loud the stockwhips crack.
Their flying course they change.
"Steadily does it—let Sambo go!
Open those sliprails down below.
Smart! or you'll be too late.
They'll follow old Sambo up—look out!
Wheel that black horse—give Sam a clout,
They're in! Make fast the gate."

The mob is safely in the yard;
The old man mounts delighted guard.
No eyes had he but for his prize.
Jim catches poor Amelia's eyes.
"Will you come with me after all I've done?
Here's Crazy Jane is fit to run
For a prince's life—now, don't say no;
Slip on while the old man's down below
At the inner yard, and away we'll go.
Will you come, my girl?" "I will, you bet,
We'll manage this here elopement yet."

By the winding Wollondilly stands the hut of Ringer Jim.
And his loving little Meely makes a perfect god of him.
He has stalwart sons and daughters, and, I think, before he's done,
There'll be numerous "six-fortys" taken on Mylora Run.

THIRSTY ISLAND

APRIL 1902

As the traveller approaches any bush township he is sure to meet, at some distance from the main town, a lonely public house waiting by the roadside to give him welcome. Thirsty (miscalled Thursday) Island is the outlying pub of Australia.

As the China and British-India steamers arrive from the north the first place they come to is Thirsty Island, sitting like a sentinel at the gate of the Torres Straits. The new chums on the steamers see a fleet of white-sailed pearling luggers, a long pier clustered with a hybrid crowd of every colour, caste and creed under Heaven, and back of it all a little galvanised iron town shining in the sun. For nine months of the year a crisp, cool south-east wind blows: the snow-white beach is splashed with spray and dotted with the picturesque figures of Japanese divers and South Sea Island boatmen. Coconut palms line the roads by the beach, and back of the town are the barracks and a fort nestled in among the trees on the hillside. Thirsty Island is a nice place—to look at.

When the vessel makes fast, the Thirsty Islanders come down to greet the newcomers and give them their welcome to Australia. The new chums are inclined to patronise these poor outlying people, who apparently are such simple folk. Fresh from the iniquities of the China coast cocktail and the unhallowed orgies of the Sourabaya Club, the new chums think that they have little to learn in the way of drink, and that, at any rate, they haven't come all the way to Thursday Island to be taught anything. Poor new chums! Little do they know the kind of people they are up against.

The following description of a night at Thirsty Island is taken verbatim from a new chum's notebook.

"Passed Proudfoot shoal and arrived at Thursday Island. First sight of Australia. Lot of men came aboard, all called Captain. They are all pearl fishers or pilots, not a bit like bushmen as I expected. When they came aboard they divided into parties. Some invaded the Captain's cabin; others sat in the smoking room; the rest crowded into the saloon. They talked to the passengers about the Boer War, and told us about pearls worth £1,000 that had been found lately. One captain pulled a handful of loose pearls out of a jar and handed them round in a casual way for us to look at. The stewards opened drinks and we all sat down for a drink and a smoke. I spoke to one captain—an oldish man—and he grinned amiably, but did not answer. Another captain leaned over to me and said, 'Don't take any notice of him, he's been boozed all this week.' Conversation and drink became general. The night was very hot and close, and some of the passengers seemed to be taking more than was good for them. A kind of contagious thirst spread round the ship, and before long the stewards and firemen were at it. The saloon became an inferno of drink and sweat and tobacco smoke. Perfect strangers were talking to each other

at the top of their voices. Young MacTavish, who is in a crack English regiment, was asking the captain of a pearling lugger whether he didn't know Talbot de Cholmondeley in the Blues, and the pearler said very likely he had met 'em, and no doubt he'd remember their faces if he saw them, but he never could remember names. Another passenger—a Jew—was trying to buy some pearls cheap from the captains, but the more the captains drank the less anxious they became to talk about pearls. The night wore on, and still the drinks circulated. Young MacTavish slept profoundly. One passenger gave his steward a sovereign, as he was leaving the ship, and in half an hour the steward was carried to his berth in a fit—the fit being alcoholic in its origin. Another steward was observed openly drinking the passengers' whisky. When accused, he didn't even attempt to defend himself—the great Thursday Island thirst seemed to have communicated itself to everyone on board, and he simply *had* to drink. About three in the morning a tour of the ship disclosed the following state of affairs: captains' room full of captains gravely and solemnly tight; smoking room empty, except for the inanimate form of the captain who had been boozed all the week, and who was now sleeping peacefully with his feet on the sofa and his head on the floor. The saloon full of captains and passengers—the latter mostly in a state of collapse or laughing and singing in a delirium of drink; the rails lined with firemen who had business over the side; stewards ditto; then at last the Thursday Islanders departed, unsteadily, but still on their feet, leaving a demoralised ship behind them. And young MacTavish, who has seen many messroom drunks, staggered to his berth, saying, 'My God! Is *all* Australia like this place?'"

When no ships arrive, the Islanders just drop into the pubs, as a matter of routine, for their usual evening soak. They drink weird compounds sometimes—horehound beer, known as "lady dog", and things like that. About two in the morning they go home speechless, but still able to travel. It is very rarely that any Islander gets helplessly drunk, but strangers generally have to be put to bed.

The Japanese on the island are a strong faction. They have a club of their own, and lately held a dinner to mark the death of one of their members. It seems he was shrewdly suspected of having tried to drown another member by cutting his air pipe, so, when he died, the club celebrated the event. The Japanese are not looked upon with favour by the white islanders. They send their money to Japan—thousands of pounds go through this little office in a year, in money orders—and so they are not "good for trade". The Manila men and kanakas and Torres Strait Islanders, on the other hand, bring all the money that they do not spend on the pearling schooners to the island, and "blow it in", like men. They knife each other sometimes, and now and again they have to be run in wholesale, but they are "good for trade". The local lock-up has a record of eighteen drunks being run in in seven minutes. They weren't taken along in carriages and four, either; they were dragged along by the scruff of the neck mostly.

Billy Malkeela, the South Sea diver, summed up the Japanese question—"Seems to me dis Islan' soon b'long Japanee altogedder. One time pa-lenty rickatta [plenty regatta], all same Isle o' Wight. Now no more rickatta. All money go Japan!"

An English new chum made his appearance here lately—a most undefeated sportsman. He was put down in a diving dress in about eight feet of water, where he bubbled and struggled about in great style. Suddenly he turned and made a rush for the beach and an ebony wit suggested that he was going up to see the diver's wife. He made for the foot of a tree, and was trying to climb it under the impression that he was still at the bottom of the ocean, when he was hauled in by the life line. The pearlers thought to get some fun out of him by giving him an oyster to open in which they had previously planted a pearl; he never saw the pearl and threw the oyster into the scuppers with the rest, and the pearlers had to go down on all fours and grope for that pearl among the stinking oysters. It was funny—but not in the way they had intended.

The pearlers go out in schooners called floating stations (their enemies call them floating public houses), and no man knows what hospitality is till he has been a guest on a pearling schooner. They carry it to extremes sometimes. Some pearlers were out in a lugger, and were passing by one of these schooners. They determined not to go on board, as it was late, and they were in a hurry. The captain of the schooner went below and got his rifle and put two bullets through their foresail. Then they put the helm down and went aboard; it was an invitation almost equivalent to a royal command. They felt heartily ashamed of themselves as they slunk up on deck, and the captain of the schooner eyed them reproachfully. "I couldn't let you disgrace yourselves by passing my schooner," he said, "but if it ever happens again I'll fire at the deck. A man that would pass a schooner in broad daylight is better dead."

There is a fort and garrison at Thirsty Island but they are not needed. If an invading fleet comes this way it should be encouraged by every possible means to land at the island; then the heat, the thirst, the horehound beer, and the Islanders may be trusted to do the rest.

A Bush Christening

DECEMBER 1893

On the outer Barcoo where the churches are few,
   And men of religion are scanty,
On a road never cross'd 'cept by folk that are lost,
   One Michael Magee had a shanty.

Now this Mike was the dad of a ten-year-old lad,
   Plump, healthy, and stoutly conditioned;
He was strong as the best, but poor Mike had no rest
   For the youngster had never been christened.

And his wife used to cry, "If the darlin' should die
   Saint Peter would not recognise him."
But by luck he survived till a preacher arrived,
   Who agreed straightaway to baptise him.

Now the artful young rogue, while they held their collogue,
   With his ear to the keyhole was listenin',
And he muttered in fright while his features turned white,
   "What the divil and all is this christenin'?"

He was none of your dolts, he had seen them brand colts,
   And it seemed to his small understanding,
If the man in the frock made him one of the flock,
   It must mean something very like branding.

So away with a rush he set off for the bush,
   While the tears in his eyelids they glistened—
"'Tis outrageous," said he, "to brand youngsters like me,
   I'll be dashed if I'll stop to be christened!"

Like a young native dog he ran into a log,
   And his father with language uncivil,
Never heeding the "praste" cried aloud in his haste,
   "Come out and be christened, you divil!"

But he lay there as snug as a bug in a rug,
   And his parents in vain might reprove him,
Till his reverence spoke (he was fond of a joke)
   "I've a notion," says he, "that'll move him.

"Poke a stick up the log, give the spalpeen a prog;
   Poke him aisy—don't hurt him or maim him,
'Tis not long that he'll stand, I've the water at hand,
   As he rushes out this end I'll name him.

"Here he comes, and for shame! ye've forgotten the name—
   Is it Patsy or Michael or Dinnis?"
Here the youngster ran out, and the priest gave a shout—
   "Take your chance, anyhow, wid 'Maginnis'!"

As the howling young cub ran away to the scrub
   Where he knew that pursuit would be risky,
The priest, as he fled, flung a flask at his head
   That was labelled "Maginnis's Whisky!"

And Maginnis Magee has been made a J.P.,
   And the one thing he hates more than sin is
To be asked by the folk who have heard of the joke,
   How he came to be christened "Maginnis"!

THE DAYLIGHT IS DYING

OCTOBER 1895

The daylight is dying
　Away in the west,
The wild birds are flying
　In silence to rest;
In leafage and frondage
　Where shadows are deep,
They pass to its bondage—
　The kingdom of sleep.
And watched in their sleeping
　By stars in the height,
They rest in your keeping,
　Oh, wonderful night.

When night doth her glories
　Of starshine unfold,
'Tis then that the stories
　Of bushland are told.
Unnumbered I hold them,
　In memories bright,
But who could unfold them,
　Or read them aright?
Beyond all denials
　The stars in their glories
The breeze in the myalls
　Are part of these stories.
The waving of grasses,
　The song of the river

That sings as it passes
　For ever and ever,
The hobble chains rattle,
　The calling of birds,
The lowing of cattle
　Must blend with the words.
Without these, indeed, you
　Would find it ere long,
As though I should read you
　The words of a song
That lamely would linger
　When lacking the rune,
The voice of the singer,
　The lilt of the tune.

But, as one half-hearing
　An old-time refrain,
With memory clearing,
　Recalls it again,
These tales, roughly wrought of
　The bush and its ways,
May call back a thought of
　The wandering days,
And, blending with each
　In the mem'ries that throng,
There haply shall reach
　You some echo of song.

LAST WEEK

DECEMBER 1893

Oh, the new chum went to the backblock run,
But he should have gone there last week.
He tramped ten miles with a loaded gun,
But of turkey or duck he saw never a one,
For he should have been there last week,
  They said,
There were flocks of 'em there last week.

He wended his way to a waterfall,
And he should have gone there last week.
He carried a camera, legs and all,
But the day was hot, and the stream was small,
For he should have gone there last week,
  They said,
They drowned a man there last week.

He went for a drive, and he made a start,
Which should have been made last week,
For the old horse died of a broken heart;
So he footed it home and he dragged the cart—
But the horse was all right last week,
  They said,
He trotted a match last week.

So he asked the bushies who came from far
To visit the town last week,
If they'd dine with him, and they said, "Hurrah!"
But there wasn't a drop in the whisky jar—
"You should have been here last week,"
  He said,
"I drank it all up last week!"

THE PANNIKIN POET

MAY 1892

There's nothing here sublime,
But just a roving rhyme,
Run off to pass the time,
  With nought titanic in
The theme that it supports
And, though it treats of quarts,
It's bare of golden thoughts—
  It's just a pannikin.

I think it's rather hard
That each Australian bard—
Each wan, poetic card—
  With thoughts galvanic in
His fiery soul alight,
In wild aerial flight,
Will sit him down and write
  About a pannikin.

He makes some new chum fare
From out his English lair
To hunt the native bear,
  That curious mannikin;
And then when times get bad
That wand'ring English lad
Writes out a message sad
  Upon his pannikin:

"Oh, mother, think of me
Beneath the wattle tree."
(For you may bet that he
  Will drag the wattle in.)
"Oh, mother, here I think
That I shall have to sink
There ain't a single drink
  The water bottle in."

The dingo homeward hies,
The sooty crows uprise
And caw their fierce surprise
  A tone Satanic in;
And bearded bushmen tread
Around the sleeper's head—
"See here—the bloke is dead."
  "Now, where's his pannikin?"

They read his words and weep,
And lay him down to sleep
Where wattle branches sweep
  A style mechanic in;
And, reader, that's the way
The poets of today
Spin out their little lay
  About a pannikin.

DIMENSIONS OF PAINTINGS

"Mulga Bill's Bicycle", **Mulga Bill and the Bicycle**—91.5 x 122 cm
"The Swagman's Rest", **The Sundowner**—61 x 91.5 cm
    Mining the Swagman's Rest—91.5 x 122 cm
"The Man from Snowy River", **The Man from Snowy River**—122 x 150 cm
    Awaiting the Verdict—91.5 x 122 cm
    Clancy on the Wing—91.5 x 122 cm
"In Re a Gentleman, One", **Winning Dream**—76 x 91.5 cm
"The Travelling Post Office", **The Letter**—76 x 61 cm
    The Outback Mailman—51 x 71 cm
"The Old Station", **The Breakaway**—51 x 66 cm
    The Homecoming—61 x 76 cm
    Finders, Keepers—61 x 76 cm
    The Breakers—61 x 76 cm
"The Old Australian Ways", **Firepower**—76 x 91.5 cm
    Saddling Up—76 x 91.5 cm
    On the Drover's Track—61 x 76 cm
"The Great Calamity", **Planning for the 50 Gallon Keg**—75 x 90 cm

"The Man from Ironbark", **The Joke's Over!**—122 x 150 cm
"Hay and Hell and Booligal", **Who Won?**—91.5 x 122 cm
    The Champ and the Challenger—91.5 x 122 cm
"Sitting in Judgment", **The Lady Riders**—61 x 76 cm
    The Champion—76 x 91.5 cm
"Father Riley's Horse", **The Horse Thief**—76 x 91.5 cm
    Buryin' Andy Regan—76 x 91.5 cm
    The Pious Dog Poisoner—76 x 91.5 cm
"The Merino Sheep", **Starting the End Run**—150 x 122 cm
"The Mylora Elopement", **Caught!**—76 x 91.5 cm
    The Proposal—91.5 x 122 cm
"Thirsty Island", **Today's Diver**—153 x 122 cm
"A Bush Christening", **The Visiting Priest**— 91.5 x 76 cm
"The Daylight Is Dying", **Pioneer Family**—76 x 91.5 cm
"Last Week", **The New Chum's Revenge**—91.5 x 76 cm
"The Pannikin Poet", **Where's His Pannikin?**—76 x 91.5 cm